Growing Up without My Daddy

A book to remind little girls that they are love, loved, and lovable,
even in the absence of their daddy

Written by Angela Adley

Illustrated by Susan Shorter

Archway Publishing books may be ordered through booksellers or by contacting:

Archway Publishing
1663 Liberty Drive
Bloomington, IN 47403
www.archwaypublishing.com
1-(888)-242-5904

Because of the dynamic nature of the Internet, any web addresses or links contained in this book may have changed since publication and may no longer be valid. The views expressed in this work are solely those of the author and do not necessarily reflect the views of the publisher, and the publisher hereby disclaims any responsibility for them.

Certain stock imagery © Thinkstock.
Any people depicted in stock imagery provided by Thinkstock are models, and such images are being used for illustrative purposes only.

ISBN: 978-1-4808-1262-8 (e)
ISBN: 978-1-4808-1261-1 (hc)
ISBN: 978-1-4808-1293-2 (sc)

Printed in the United States of America.

Archway Publishing rev. date: 12/9/2014

This Book Belongs To:

_____

I want to thank God for His grace, His mercy, His blessings, and for guiding me to carry out the passion that He placed in my heart to share my story.

I want to thank my beautiful mother, Tamara Dawson, for her unconditional love and support.

I want to thank my father, Ken Adley, for loving me and trying to carve out a relationship with me the best way he knew how.

I want to thank my maternal and paternal grandparents, who are angels resting above, for always making me feel special.

I want to thank my God sent grandmother, Gertrude Lawson, for loving me to pieces and always guiding me toward God's spirit.

I want to thank Angela Carr Patterson for believing in me, inspiring me on my journey to healing my daddy wounds, and coaching me to achieve peace at heart so that I could speak from my truest voice and live out my truest desires.

I want to thank Rev. Dr. Della Reese Lett for assisting me in learning and understanding the universal principles for better living so that I could release the divine potential within me.

I want to thank Rev. Dr. Leslie D. Braxton for encouraging me to stop sitting on my testimony, as well as for reminding me that God was aiming for something when he divinely designed me and that I am responsible for fulfilling God's purpose.

I want to thank Terrance R. Metcalf II for the opportunity to experience what it feels like and what it means to really love and show up fully in love, even when there may be no next time, no time-outs, or second chances.

I also want to thank close friends Li-Ling Li, Ericka Singh, Cerise Barton, Chanda Sanders, and Tonia Hogan for bringing so much love and laughter along my path.

It's not failure, it's a lesson, and if you learn from it and keep going, failure can be a great teacher.

—MASTIN KIPP

Each day we are born again. What we do today is what matters most.

—BUDDHA

True forgiveness is when you can say "Thank you for that experience."

—OPRAH WINFREY

In the flush of love's light we dare be brave and suddenly we see that love costs all we are and will ever be. Yes, it is only love which sets us free.

—MAYA ANGELOU

My daddy is absent
from my life.

My daddy doesn't live at my
house, take me to school,
or pick me up from school.

My daddy doesn't cook for me, take me to play with my friends, or take me to tap dancing class.

TAP DANCE SCHOOL

My daddy is also not
here to help me with
my homework or to help
me look for my lost toys.

My daddy does not play dolls with me or have tea parties with me.

My daddy also does not
tuck me into bed at
night nor does he tell
me bedtime stories.

My daddy is also not here to tickle me, hug me, kiss me, hold my hand, or even tell me, "I love you." When I fall down and get hurt or when someone makes me sad or angry, my daddy is not here for me to tell.

I miss my daddy, and I wish he were a part of my life. It makes me feel very sad that he's not with me like other daddies. Sometimes, I don't feel loved, secure, or wanted, even though my mommy and grandparents shower me with lots of love.

However, I am learning that my daddy loves me the best way he knows how, and I am to love, accept, and forgive him for not being a part of my life the way that I would like him to be.

It is very hard to do all of this because I am just a little girl, but I am learning that God is my true Father.

My very existence shows God's love for me, and because I know that, I now feel completely loved and completely lovable.

I love myself through the love reflected in God and who God says I am. God tells me I am made in His image and likeness. Thus, all that my Father is, I am.

So who am I? I am love;
I am completely loved and
completely lovable. And so
are YOU!!! Always know
and believe that you too ARE
LOVE, LOVED, AND LOVABLE
BECAUSE GOD SAYS YOU ARE!!!

BELIEVE IN YOU!!!

PLACE YOUR PHOTO HERE:

DRAW A PICTURE OF YOURSELF HERE:

WHO IS YOUR TRUE FATHER?

_____

_____

_____

_____

_____

_____

_____

_____

_____

_____

_____

WHO DOES GOD SAY YOU ARE?

_____

_____

_____

_____

_____

_____

_____

_____

_____

_____

_____

WHO DO YOU SAY YOU ARE?

_____

_____

_____

_____

_____

_____

_____

_____

_____

_____

_____

HOW DO YOU KNOW YOU ARE LOVE, LOVED, AND LOVABLE?

_____

_____

_____

_____

_____

_____

_____

_____

_____

_____

ANGELA ADLEY is a pediatric speech-language pathologist residing in Seattle, Washington. She recently became a certified fatherless daughter advocate through Angela Carr Patterson's Journey to Being System, which inspired this personal story to assist young girls in filling the void of growing up fatherless.

Printed in the United States
by Baker & Taylor Publisher Services